# Objects from the Tibetan Lamaist Collection of Jacques Marchais

**511449**

*To*

*Harry*

*Whose constant encouragement*

*has been a source of inspiration.*

THE LATE PANCHAN LAMA OF TIBET

# *Foreword*

IN THIS BROCHURE I am not attempting to give full identifications, iconography or mythology of the ritual pieces and figures herein reproduced. My object, at this time, is merely a response to the many requests that have been made by visitors to my gallery, for large photographic reproductions of a few of the silver and gilt-bronze deities, symbols and altar equipage, that are a part of my large Tibetan collection. It is my intention to publish a book sometime in the near future, which will deal fully with the whole group of Tibetan objects, assembled by my great-grandfather and myself.

I feel that it is now most appropriate to proffer this brochure, because I have recently received from the Orient, the silver set of Tantric Dharmapala ritual implements that were used by His Serene Holiness, the late Panchan Lama, when he presented the religious ceremonies in China, that were to exorcise the Japanese out of Chinese territory.

For more than a year I have been negotiating with men of good repute, in China and Mongolia—striving to obtain a few of the personal things that had belonged to the Panchan Lama. At long last, they have arrived on our shores, and are in my possession. I have every reason to believe that they are authentic. At some future time I shall tell the interesting story, how these things were obtained, and of the intrigue and daring used by those who helped negotiate for them.

The late Panchan Lama of North Tibet was exiled to China by his old arch-enemy, the late and thirteenth Dalai-Lama.

In 1931, the Chinese were paying him $586,000 a year to consolidate the Tibetan Border States — and to arouse pro-Chinese sentiment among the Buddhists of the world. The Chinese Government provided him with a beautiful Rolls-Royce motor-car, that was upholstered in yellow velvet, and a yellow train which was the last word in modern equipment and luxury.

With his large and expensive entourage, he presented one of the most splendid and colorful ceremonial pageants ever produced anywhere in the world. It was held in the Temple-that-Flew-over-from-India, located at Hang-Chow. For two weeks the Panchan Lama presided in person over the public prayers and services dedicated to the peace of the world—using these ritual pieces in many of the ceremonies—and in others, a duplicate set of solid gold.

When he personally took part in these services, he wore the handsome costumes that had been made by command of the Emperor Chien-Lung (1736-1796), for the Panchan Lama of that era.

The Panchan Lama is the spiritual ruler of Lamaism—the living Lord Buddha—Amitabha. It is a position which is religiously the highest in the Tibetan theocracy.

*Jacques Marchais*

April 12, 1941

(T.) SNA-TS'OGS RDO-RJE

(s.) Visvavajra

Double or Crossed Thunderbolt

This symbol is the Tibetan Lamaist crossed dorje, and it is symbolical of Power, Balance and Permanence.

(T.) Indicates Tibetan names or phonetic pronunciation.
(s.) Is the Sanskrit.

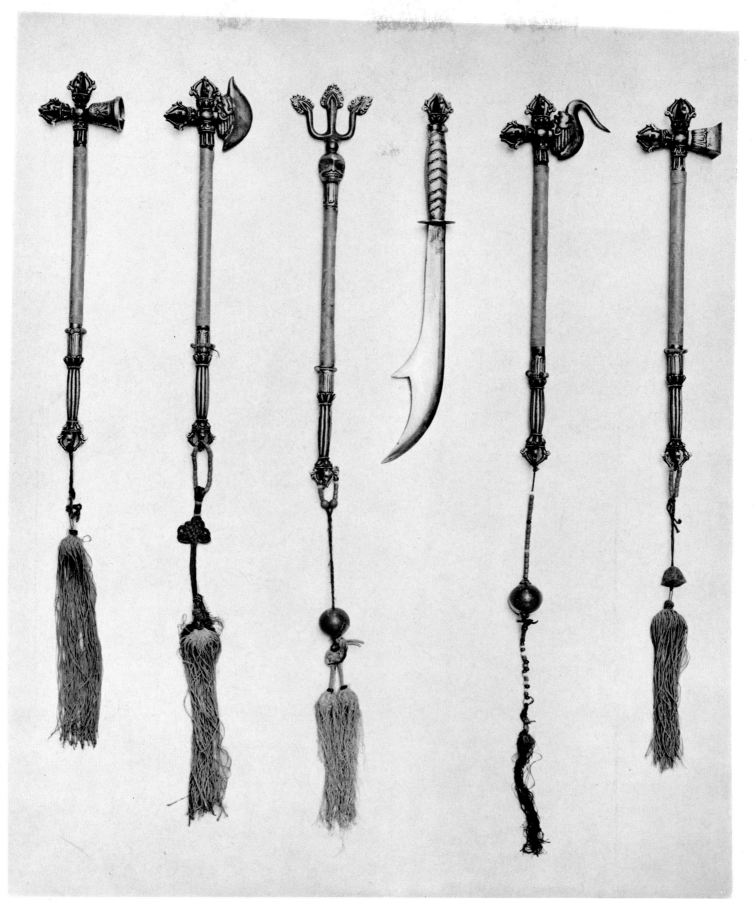

THE LATE PANCHAN LAMA'S SILVER RITUAL IMPLEMENTS

|   |   | *Tibetan* | *Sanskrit* |
|---|---|---|---|
| 1. | The Bell | DRIL-BU | Ghanta |
| 2. | The Axe | DGRA-STA | Parasu |
| 3. | The Trident | K'A-'TVAN-RTSE-GSUM | Trisula |
| 4. | The Knife | GRI | Chu-gri |
| 5. | The Goad | LC'AGS-KYU | Ankusa |
| 6. | The Hammer | T'O-BA MT'O-BA | Mudgara |

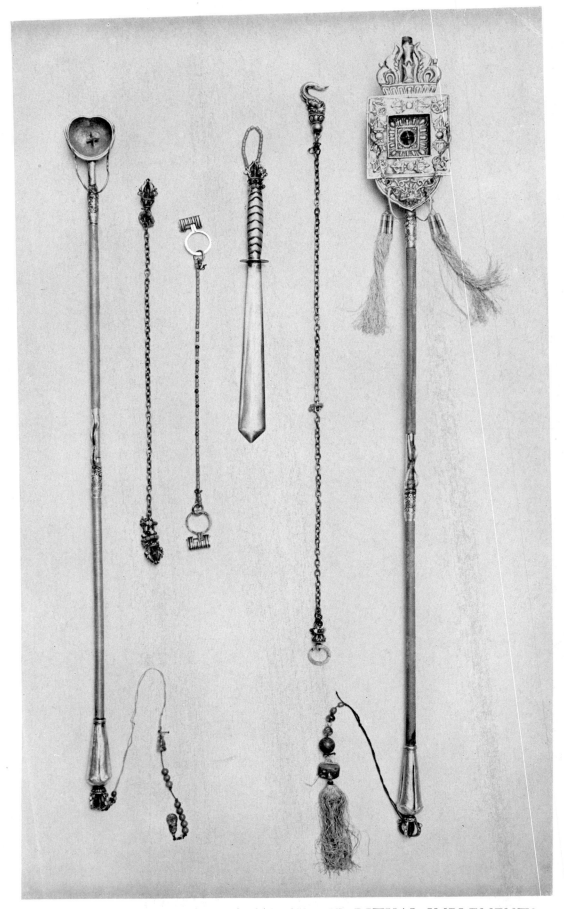

## THE LATE PANCHAN LAMA'S SILVER RITUAL IMPLEMENTS
(*continued*)

|     |                                              | *Tibetan* | *Sanskrit* |
| --- | -------------------------------------------- | --------- | ---------- |
| 7.  | Ladle                                        | T'UM-BU   | Darvika    |
| 8.  | Noose—with half dorje at each end            | Z'AGS-PA  | Pasa       |
| 9.  | Noose—with padlock at each end               | Z'AGS-PA  | Pasa       |
| 10. | Sword                                        | RAL-GRI   | adi        |
| 11. | Noose—with ring at one end and hook at other | Z'AGS-PA  | Pasa       |
| 12. | Anointing implement                          | ?         | ?          |

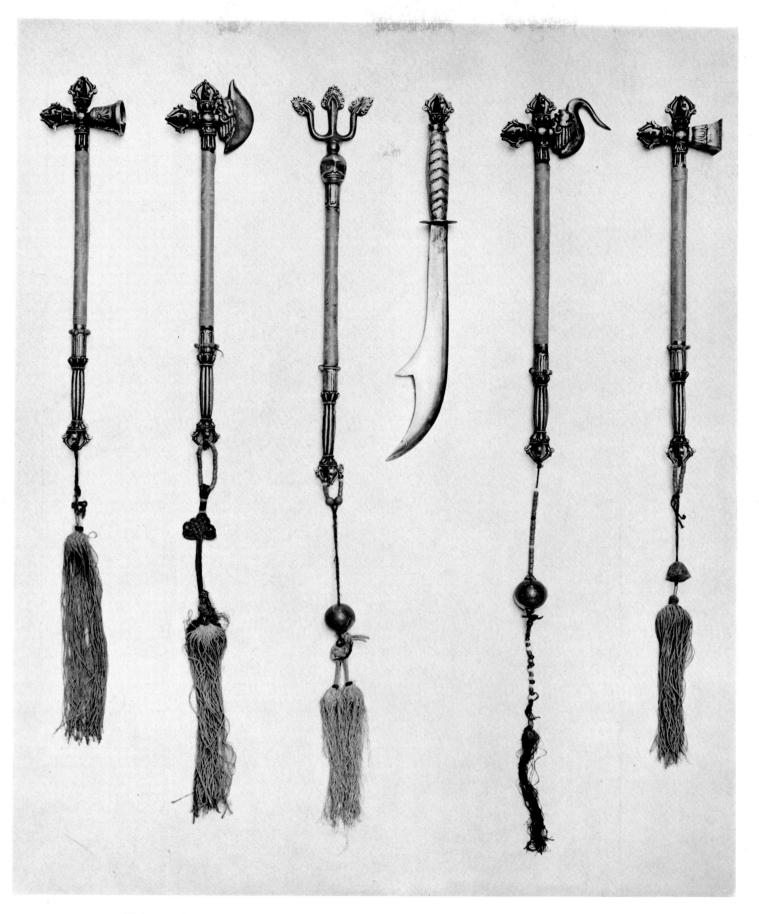

## THE LATE PANCHAN LAMA'S SILVER RITUAL IMPLEMENTS

|   | | Tibetan | Sanskrit |
|---|---|---|---|
| 1. | The Bell | DRIL-BU | Ghanta |
| 2. | The Axe | DGRA-STA | Parasu |
| 3. | The Trident | K'A-'TVAN-RTSE-GSUM | Trisula |
| 4. | The Knife | GRI | Chu-gri |
| 5. | The Goad | LC'AGS-KYU | Ankusa |
| 6. | The Hammer | T'O-BA MT'O-BA | Mudgara |

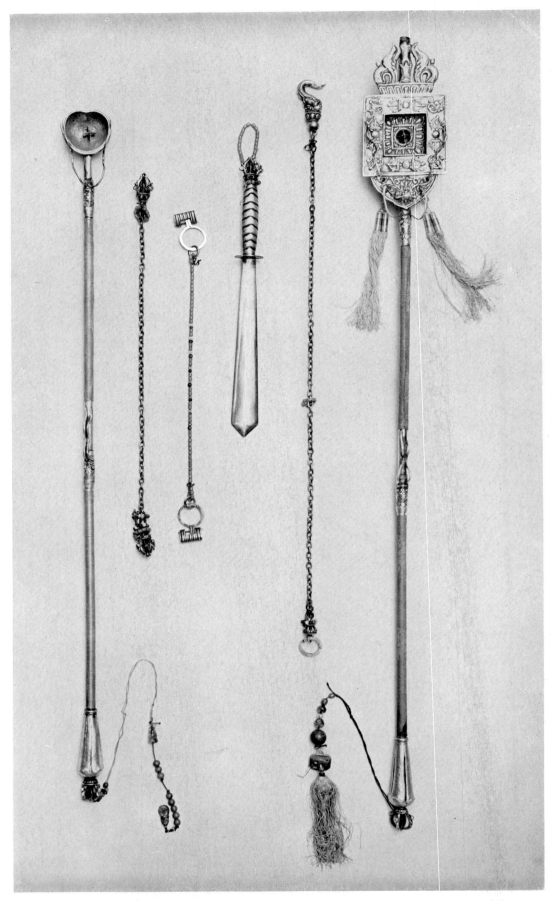

## THE LATE PANCHAN LAMA'S SILVER RITUAL IMPLEMENTS

*(continued)*

| | | Tibetan | Sanskrit |
|---|---|---|---|
| 7. | Ladle | T'UM-BU | Darvika |
| 8. | Noose—with half dorje at each end | Z'AGS-PA | Pasa |
| 9. | Noose—with padlock at each end | Z'AGS-PA | Pasa |
| 10. | Sword | RAL-GRI | adi |
| 11. | Noose—with ring at one end and hook at other | Z'AGS-PA | Pasa |
| 12. | Anointing implement | ? | ? |

## (T.) P'UR-BU
### (S.) Phurbu
#### (LIT.) "Peg or Nail"

This is an elongated dagger with the pointed blade
spreading into a triangle up to the hilt. There is usu-
ally a head in the upper part of the handle, which is
believed to be Hayagriva. He is venerated in Tibet
as a very special protector against evil spirits.

## (T.) RKAN-GLIN

### Thigh-bone Trumpet

This trumpet is made from a human thigh-bone,
banded in silver and studded with coral and turquoise.
Waddell tells us that—"In the preparation of these
thigh-bone trumpets the bones of criminals or those
who have died by violence are preferred."

(T.) T'OD-K'RAG

(S.) Kapala

Skull-cup

In this container is placed a preparation, sometimes black tea, sometimes grain brandy, or it may be water, colored red like blood, the concoction representing the beverage of immortality. This libation is then offered to the Gods. In early times, when the Pon influence was strong, the blood of animals was used.

(т.)  P R E N - B A

(s.)  Mala

Rosary

This rosary was removed from around the neck of a very old figure of the God Yama.

The beads are made of human bone—and the nine heads are of copper; four are painted green, two red and three white; these being interspersed between the beads.

(I.)  K'AR - RNA

Gong

This hand gong is of silver—and used during temple services.

(s.) Kapala

Skull Bowl

This skull bowl is used for offerings. It is lined with heavy silver and studded with turquoise and coral.

(T.)  R N A - Y A B

(s.)  Camara

Fly-whisk

The fly-whisk is used in Tantric services.

(T.) K'RUS-BUM

Holy-water Vase

This vase is of silver, and the workmanship is very beautiful.

When in use on a lama altar, it would be filled with saffron water. The peacock's feathers with the holy kusa grass are used to sprinkle the water upon the offerings, etc., during a service.

## TIBETAN INCENSE BURNER

This burner is made of copper and silver.

## LIBATION JUG

This jug is made of copper. The tip of the spout and the fangs of the creature on the handle are silver.

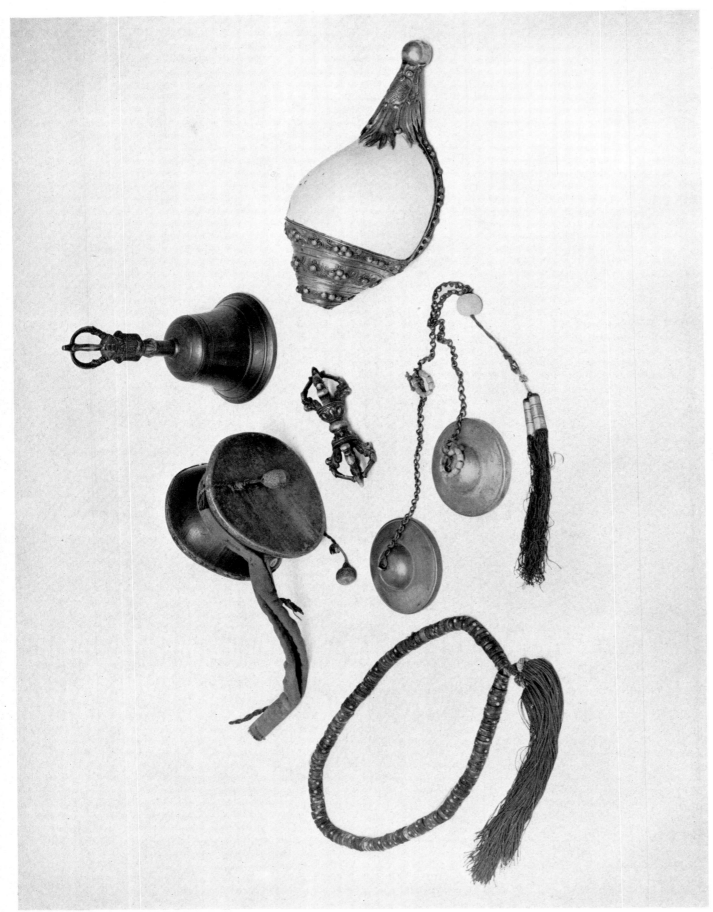

A GROUP OF RITUAL PIECES
(Used on a Tantric Altar)

ROSARY
(t.) PREN-BA    (s.) Mala

CONCH-SHELL TRUMPET
(t.) DUN    (s.) Sankha

DRUM
(t.) DA-MA-RU    (s.) Damaru

CYMBALS
(t.) ROL-MO

BELL
(t.) DRIL-BU    (s.) Ghanta

THUNDERBOLT
(t.) RDO-RJE or DORJE
(s.) Vajra

(T.) MANI CHHO-KHOR
(s.) Dharma-chakra
Prayer-wheel

This Tibetan cylinder contains a large roll of prayers printed on paper, and the usual formula—"Om Mani Padme Hum" (the literal meaning, "Om! The Jewel in the Lotus! Hum!"), is used.

The term "Prayer-wheel" being now so generally used—does not, as I understand it, give the correct meaning or sense to the phrase. Sir Alexander Cunningham (now deceased) called them Mani-chhos-Kor; and he translated it—"The Precious Religious Wheel."

(T.)  M C H ' O D - S K O N

(S.)  Dipah

Lamp

A very fine old silver altar lamp.  Melted butter is burned in these containers; and a wealthy monastery would have 108 or more lamps burning at a time on its altar.

## TIBETAN BUTTER CONTAINER

This container is placed near a Tibetan altar—and, from it the Lamas dip butter to replenish the butter lamps. It is made of wood, the ornaments of gilt copper, and here and there it is jeweled.

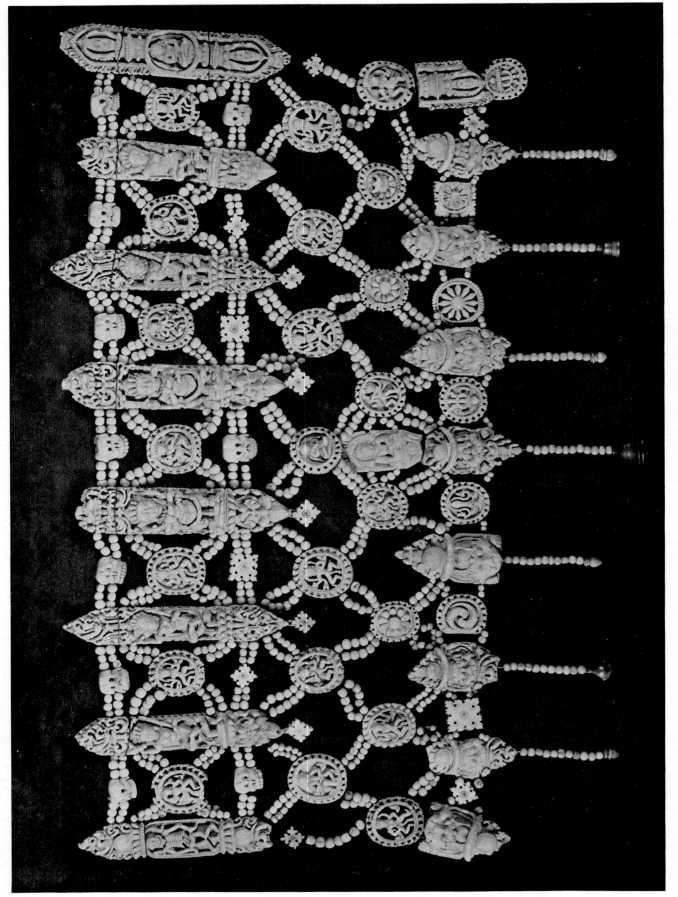

APRON OF CARVED HUMAN BONES

Sanmudras

(Human Bones)

Used by Black Hat Priests in Necromantic Rites.

## LIBATION AND TIBETAN TEA JUGS

The two Libation jugs stand near the altar—ready to refill bowls with holy water. The tall insulated tea jug (shown in the centre) is insulated to keep the tea hot for hours; and it is a good forerunner of the modern thermos-bottle of the Western World. All three vessels are of copper.

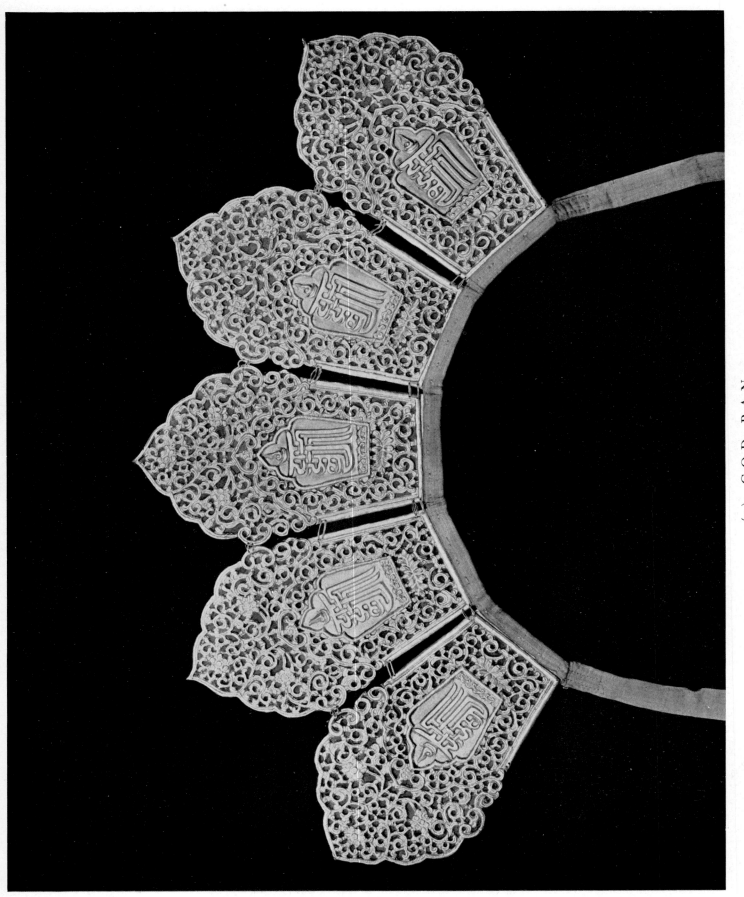

(T.)  C O D - P A N

(S.)  Cho-pen

Five-Leaved Crown

This crown is made of silver and has the Mystic Monogram  (rNam-behu-dvang-ldan)  "The All-powerful Ten," in each leaf of the crown.

## (T.)  B D E - M C H ' O G  (*Yi-dam*)

### (S.)  Samvara

Samvara is known as the chief of happiness—also called dpal-'k'or-lo-sdom-pa.  As Yi-dam he has the rank of Buddha.
The Tibetans believe him to be a mystical deity who, according to the formula dedicated to him—"Sprang from a combination of all the letters of the alphabet."

His color is blue.  His four heads have their own individual color, and if they are painted, the central one is blue; the one at the right should be white; the one at the left, green; and the one at the back, red.

He is here shown with his sakti, Vagravrahi.  She is of a cherry color.  Her name means the "adamantine sow."

(r.) GSIN-RJE-GSED

(s.) Yamantaka (*Dharmapala*)

Destroyer of the Lord of Death (Yama).

Yamantaka destroyed the God of Death, who was exterminating the people of Tibet, in his wild lust for creatures to sacrifice to his own glorification.

(T.) PHYI-SGRUB

(S.) Yama (*Dharmapala*)

Minister of the Exterior

We are told that, before the great reformer, Tson-Ka-pa passed on, he designated Yama as the protector of the Ge-lugs-pa sect ("Yellow Hats").

He is represented standing on a bull, under which is a woman. He is accompanied by his sister Yami.

## (т.) L H A - M O (*Dharmapala*)
### (s.) sri-devi
### "The Goddess"

This terrifying goddess is the only feminine deity among the "Eight Terrible Ones."

The legend concerning her relates that she made a vow to kill her son, and put an end to the royal race, if she did not succeed in converting her husband and her people to Buddhism. All her efforts to no avail, she 'flayed her son alive, drank his blood and ate his flesh.' The king, her husband, became so enraged that he shot an arrow off at her and her mount. It hit and imbedded itself in the haunch of her mule. Upon her pulling it out, a great eye manifested itself in the spot where the wound should have been. Many and varied are the tales concerning her. She is regarded as the Protectress of the Dalai-Lama of Tibet. When painted her color is blue and that of her mule is white.

(T.) MGON-PO

(S.) Mahakala (*Dharmapala*)

"Protector of Tents"

May be represented in innumerable forms. One example of which is that where he treads on one elephant headed figure —of a human (the demon Vinataku) and another where he stands upon two figures, both having elephant's heads.

(т.) R T A - M G R I N  (*ch'os-skyon*)

(s.) Hayagriva (*Dharmapala*)

This is an unusually fine figure, too fine to be left out of this group, even though the symbols are missing from the hands; their having been lost in transit, on the way to the gallery.  Each hand should carry one of the following symbols: a vajra, a mace, a flower, a lotus, bow and arrow and two hands should make a mystic gesture.

In Tibet he is worshipped principally by the horse-traders.  He is not the god, Protector of Horses; still it is believed that he neighs like a horse and thus frightens away demons.

Probably an aspect of—

(T.) TS'ANGS-PA DKAR-PO *(Dharmapala)*

(S.) Brahma

"White Brahma"

Very little is known about Ts'angs-pa Dkar-po.

(T.)  BEG-TS'E  (*Dharmapala*)

(lit. "hidden shirt of mail")

Protector of Horses and God of War

Very little information has been found in regard to this God, up to the present time.

511449

(т.) R N A M - T ' O S - S R A S

(s.) Kuvera (*Dharmapala*)

God of Wealth

He is one of "The Eight Terrible Ones"—but with a mild countenance, seated on a lion. The mongoose symbolizes his conquest over the Nagas (Serpent Gods).